IMAGES
of America

CARDIFF
ILLINOIS'S LOST MINING TOWN

Inside the Henry Meyers house in Cardiff in 1912 are Meyers's granddaughters Mary Roquet (left) and Alta Falk (right). Mary (Roquet) McCabe lived to the age of 100. (Author's collection.)

ON THE COVER: Cardiff had a large opera house which hosted many social events. There also were a number of halls above stores that hosted events. (Author's collection.)

IMAGES
of America

CARDIFF
ILLINOIS'S LOST MINING TOWN

Jim Ridings

ARCADIA
PUBLISHING

Published by Arcadia Publishing
Charleston, South Carolina

Printed in the United States of America

Library of Congress Control Number: 2023947587

For all general information, please contact Arcadia Publishing:
Telephone 843-853-2070
Fax 843-853-0044
E-mail sales@arcadiapublishing.com

Visit us on the Internet at www.arcadiapublishing.com

CONTENTS

ACKNOWLEDGMENTS

Thanks to the many people who supplied pictures and information. Many of these pictures have never been seen before outside of the families and might never be seen if not for the generosity of these people who were willing to share them. Essential information came from libraries, courthouse records, and government reports. All images appear courtesy of author's collection unless otherwise noted.

ABOUT THE AUTHOR

Jim Ridings was born in Joliet, Illinois. He earned a bachelor of science degree in journalism from Southern Illinois University. He was a reporter for the *Daily Times* in Ottawa and the *Beacon-News* in Aurora. He won more than a dozen awards for investigative reporting at both newspapers from the Associated Press, United Press International, and other organizations. Ridings has written and published 34 books of Illinois history, including the groundbreaking *Len Small: Governors and Gangsters*; *Small Justice*; *Cardiff: Ghost Town on the Prairie*; *County West: A Sesquicentennial History of Western Kankakee County*; *Wild Kankakee*; and *Murder in the Fox Valley*. Nine of his books have won awards from the Illinois State Historical Society. He was presented a Studs Terkel Humanities Service bronze medal from the Illinois Humanities Council in 2006. Jim and Janet Ridings live in Herscher, Illinois, and have two daughters, Stephanie and Laura, and grandchildren Declan, Mia, and Logan.

INTRODUCTION

Just before the turn of the 20th century, Livingston County, Illinois, was a quiet prairie land. There was the small town of Campus with a couple of hundred people, a number of farms, and prairie land. Then, in early 1899, a coal company prospecting for new coalfields discovered a promising vein just northeast of Campus. The company drilled a mine, and the Cardiff coal mine was in operation by the end of the year.

A relatively big town of about 1,300 people sprang up around the Cardiff mine, with houses, a school, a church, stores, and saloons.

But the good times ended abruptly on March 13, 1903, when an explosion in the mine killed three men. Several other explosions followed in the next few days, and a total of nine men were dead.

Everyone said this was the end of the town of Cardiff. But it wasn't.

Even though many miners left town, more were attracted when the coal company sank a new shaft within a few months. The boom was back on, and Cardiff grew bigger than ever, with some estimates of 2,500 people living there. It continued that way until the high-quality coal ran out, and the Wabash Railroad, its biggest customer, refused to buy the lower-quality coal.

The mine closed in 1912. Cardiff continued as a town for a few more years.

It is fascinating how a town sprang from nowhere and disappeared almost as quickly. But it also is fascinating just how much there was to Cardiff. Cardiff had two banks, two grain elevators, clothing stores, two meat markets, two bakeries, several barbershops, a millinery shop, two livery stables, several general stores, a pharmacy, two blacksmith shops, two icehouses, a doctor's office, and a real estate and insurance office. It had a soft drink bottling plant and a candy factory. It had at least two dance halls and an automobile dealership at the dawn of the automobile age.

Cardiff had a pressurized water system, a gas works system, and an electric light plant. It had a large schoolhouse and a church. Cardiff had cement sidewalks in an era when most of the established towns in the area did not. It had a railroad depot with passenger service and two railroad lines. It had a first-class hotel with fine cuisine.

Cardiff had three semiprofessional baseball teams and a first-class baseball diamond and grandstand that was one of the first in the state to have night baseball, with the diamond lit from the town's coal gas plant. There was a racetrack behind the livery stables for weekend horse racing. Cardiff also had a semipro football team, a bowling alley, and tennis courts.

Everything about Cardiff was bigger than it was in nearby towns. And there is a completeness to it: Cardiff had a beginning, a life, and an end.

The town did not really have a natural decline. As soon as the mine closed, houses were being dismantled and hauled away. Almost as quickly as the town sprang up, it vanished from the face of the earth.

While Cardiff is gone, there are still a few houses and trailers along a rural road. You can drive through and never know anything had been there. The town—streets, neighborhoods, and all—has gone back to farmland.

This book is not just the story of a mine disaster. It is the story of the people of a mining town that once were alive. For a while, they live again here.

One

COAL IS DISCOVERED

The area in northeast Livingston County was not known as Cardiff when mining began in 1899. In fact, there was not supposed to be a town there at all.

Campus was the closest town near the site, and that is where the people who worked at the mine were supposed to live.

When the White Breast Fuel Coal Company came to the area in April 1899, it wanted to start mining closer to Campus and the company was willing to pay the top price of $100 per acre. But some people in Campus did not want a coal mine close to town. They refused to sell their land, so the company started drilling a shaft two miles north.

Ground was broken for the new mine on May 6, 1899.

The influential men of Campus saw the coal mine strictly as a work site, with Campus benefiting by providing housing and stores for the workers.

The White Breast Fuel Coal Company named its subsidiary the Campus Coal Company. For the first four months during development of the mine site, the area was known as North Campus.

Within months, a grain elevator, 20 houses, and a hotel had been built. And the Wabash Railroad was running passenger trains between Campus and North Campus.

The coal company planned the town with businesses located along Wabash Avenue and Main Street; no businesses were built in residential areas. This kept the rougher elements, such as the drinkers, from where families lived.

September 1, 1899, was a big day for the town. It was the day the small, busy mining camp that had been known as North Campus was officially named Cardiff, after one of the richest coal mining areas in the world: Cardiff, Wales. The name of the company became the Cardiff Coal Company.

In Cardiff's first year, it became the top producer of the 15 mines in Livingston County. Of the 933 coal mines in the state, Cardiff was the 44th largest. In 1903, Cardiff produced 201,556 tons of coal. The next largest mine in the county was at Pontiac, with 56,650 tons. The peak year of production was 1908, when 216,987 tons of coal was mined.

A stream of light comes down the shaft from the surface in this wonderful picture of the inside of the mine.

Here, miners are loading coal into railcars.

This was the blacksmith shop at the Cardiff mine. The blacksmiths took care of the mules that pulled the coal cars from the mine.

The slack wash at the mine collected coal fragments and dirt that remained after the coal was screened. It created giant mine hills on the prairie.

Pictured from left to right, Edmund, Vincent, and Anton Berta show that coal mining was a dirty business in this look inside a mine at South Wilmington.

Mules were used to pull coal cars from the mine to the surface, as seen in this early picture of Butch Rule (left) and Leonard Hockings (right) in the nearby South Wilmington mine.

Two

THE OVERNIGHT BOOM TOWN

By mid-September 1899, approximately 200 people were working at Cardiff. On September 24, 1899, the first baby was born in Cardiff to Richard and Lizzie Savage. Her name was Sadie Savage. Sadie was born five days before her niece Elizabeth, whose parents, Ulysis and Margaret Alderson, lived in Clarke City. Both Richard Savage and his son-in-law Ulysis Alderson lost their lives in the Cardiff mine.

The coal company built houses for about $500 each and rented them to the miners for around $5 per month. The houses were painted in five colors, but no two houses of the same color were side by side.

The Livingston Supply Company, the company store, sold dry goods, meat, and drugs, and it housed a doctor's office. In many mining towns, some of the miners' pay was in the form of script, which could be spent at the company store.

The two-story Hotel DeWelcome was built on the north end of town. It was managed by Jack Price, who became manager of the Hotel Cardiff when it opened in 1900. It was the Welshman Price whose influence gave Cardiff its name.

Streets were named for people who were building Cardiff: Harry Parker, the mine superintendent; George Holt, secretary to the superintendent, paymaster, and timekeeper; L.A. Chamberlain, manager of the company store; and James Donaldson, the pit boss.

From the beginning, Cardiff showed its love for the saloons for which it became famous. The corporate line of Campus extended to Cardiff, formerly North Campus. This meant that Cardiff had to abide by the prohibition of alcohol in Campus. A meeting was held in Cardiff, and it was voted to separate from the legal boundaries of Campus.

In March 1900, enough property owners had signed a petition to have the matter of incorporation placed on the April ballot. It was approved by all 77 people who voted. The new village covered 120 acres, and it was officially incorporated on May 24, 1900. In the first village election on June 19, 1900, Frank Milem was elected mayor.

Here are two views of the Livingston Supply Company. There is a meat market sign and a mortar and pestle sign for the pharmacy of A.M. Corbus, who is on the left above. Next to him are, from left to right, Dr. Alvin Keller; an unidentified butcher; manager L.A. Chamberlain; and John McCullough, a clerk. A delivery boy is on the cart.

The company store is on the left, and Ciochetti's tavern is on the right.

The Schlitz Beer hall was on the corner of Wabash Avenue and Main Street.

This view of Wabash Avenue is looking north from Main Street in 1907. Cardiff had a variety of stores for a mining town. There are signs for Cohen's Bargain Store, a restaurant north of that, the Bank of Cardiff, and Fred E. Ahern's offices. North of the bank was H.L. Lazerowitz's store. South of Cohen's was Emile Roquet's saloon and the Schlitz saloon.

This image shows a hotel in Cardiff.

Pictured here is the inside of the Roquet saloon in Cardiff.

Even the town marshal enjoyed good times in the Roquet saloon.

Rosie Bertoncello (left) and Margaret Meyers (right) posed on the incline leading from the mine to the tipple and the rest of the mine works.

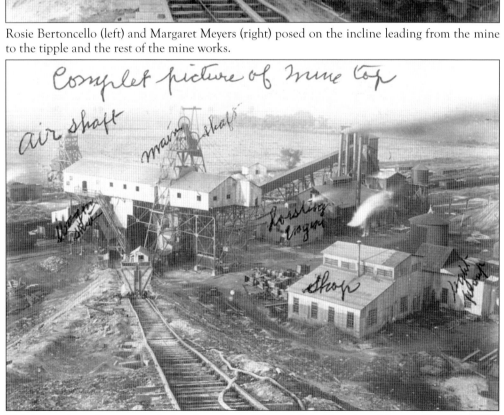

This image from the same angle has the mine buildings labeled by miner Thomas Tyrrell in 1910. It shows the air shaft, the main shaft, the wagon shop, the hoisting engine, another shop, and the light plant.

Coal mines used a lot of timber to shore up walls underground.

Cardiff's public school building was on Main Street at Holt Avenue. Identified in this picture from 1907 are Principal Thomas F. Clinton and teachers Etta Cody, Anna Walsh, and Mayme McDonald.

In this Cardiff School picture from 1909, Ward Parker is in the first row, third from the right. Mary Juricic is the third girl left of the teacher in the third row. Annie Parker is in the fourth row, fourth from the right.

This Cardiff grammar school class in 1902 identifies Goldie Meyers (fourth row, fourth from the right) and Mary Juricic (second row, fourth from the left). R.E. Carney is the teacher.

In this Cardiff School picture from 1903, R.E. Carney is the teacher. Lucy Ciochetti is in the fourth row, sixth girl from the left.

Cardiff's intermediate grades are pictured here in 1909. From left to right are (first row) Rachel Hamill, Johnny Secondino, Cecelia Baima, Charley Secondino, Pearl Snyder, William McCully, Hazel Murphy, and Esther Carlson; (second row) Leon White, Katherine Wortman, Frances Beneitone, Arthur Roquet, Jimmie Higgins, and Patrick Devlin; (third row) Emma Hreha, Edith Coskey, Caroline Wortman, Principal T.F. Clinton, Blanche Carmean, Hazel Kerns, and Marie Singer.

Pictured is a Cardiff class from 1908. In the first row is Clifford Williams (second from the right) and Wilda Parker (fifth from the right). In the second row are Marie McLean (far left) and John McLean (far right). Pauline Ballotti is below the middle window, with the white ribbon in her hair.

Harry Williams (grandson of mine superintendent Harry Parker) is in the fourth row, fifth from the left. Clifford Williams, his brother, is in the third, fifth from the left.

This was a class at Cardiff's school in 1917. Johnny Tyrrell is in the first row, third from the left. Frank Juricic is second from the right in the first row.

This was Cardiff's opera house.

The Meyers family operated this restaurant and bakery.

A station agent stands in front of the Wabash Railroad depot, with the Hotel Cardiff behind it. A train ran off the tracks in 1912, burning down the depot and the hotel.

Passengers wait on the Wabash depot platform in 1908.

Joe Roquet is in the dark suit in this picture of the Cardiff Gun Club.

This view of Wabash Avenue, south of Main Street, is looking north. The meat market is on the northeast corner, past the building labeled "tavern," which was Ciochetti's. The building on the southwest corner is Tintorri's tavern, with its advertisement for Kankakee's Radeke Beer.

This picture shows Main Street just west of town, looking east from Fred Ahern's house on the left. Thomas Tyrrell's house is indicated.

This view is from the same angle, looking west on Main Street, after the street was improved.

This picture shows the east end of Main Street, looking west from Holt Avenue. Children are playing outside a house in this picture from 1907. The school is on the right.

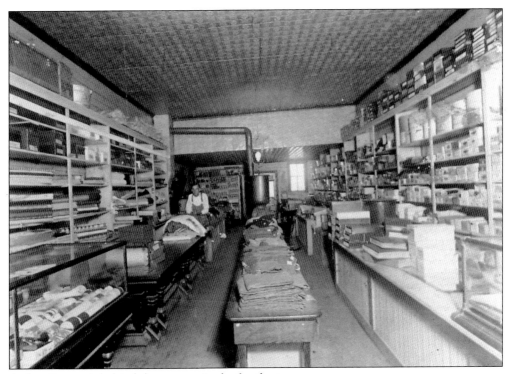

Arthur Roquet is behind the counter in the family store.

The Fred E. Ahern Baseball Association was incorporated with the state in 1908. Baseball was very popular in Cardiff, and it was very competitive. Violence sometimes erupted between fans of rival teams. Pictured above is a baseball game in 1907 in nearby Cabery. Cabery's team is pictured below.

Tokens used as cash were very common in stores and saloons all across America in the late 1800s and early 1900s. These are from Ronchetti's grocery store and Walters & Alford's saloon.

Cardiff was a mining town that was much more than its coal mine. Unlike many other mining towns, quite a few houses were privately owned rather than owned by the coal company. And the company store did not dominate local business. Most stores were privately owned.

J.D. Williams is pictured here as a coal miner at Cardiff, Wales, before coming to Cardiff, Illinois. His son Thomas married Margaret Parker, daughter of Cardiff mine superintendent Harry Parker. Thomas was killed in an explosion in the downstate Herrin mine in 1909. Margaret was three months pregnant at the time. Several of her children were raised by their Parker grandparents in Cardiff.

This view inside a coal mine is from nearby South Wilmington.

Three

DISASTER

Everything changed at midnight on Thursday, March 12, 1903. An explosion in the mine sent a huge blast of air that blew three miners against the shaft wall. Killed were Joseph Hewitt, John McClosky, and James Barra.

An accident earlier that day had disabled the hoisting engines at the mine shaft. The company used the breakdown as an opportunity to make repairs to air shafts and escape shafts in abandoned parts of the mine. All the miners had been sent home except for 15 workmen who were left to make the repairs.

The huge explosion shook the town and awakened most of the residents. Flames and debris shot more than 100 feet from the mine opening.

Funerals for the three victims were held in Cardiff on Sunday, March 15. But the mourners barely finished with the funerals when a second explosion rocked the mine at 5:30 p.m. Six men were in the mine at that time, cleaning up debris from the first blast and repairing the damage. Five of those men were killed: Anton Hasal, Anton Jeokoski, Ulysis Alderson, Archie Wilson, and James Hutchinson.

A third huge explosion shot from the mine at 9:30 a.m. on Monday, March 16. This was the largest blast of all, blowing out the top of the mine shaft and damaging machinery, the power house, and the engine house. Company carpenter Allen Michaels was looking down the mine shaft when it blew. He was hit in the chest by flying timbers and was killed. Michaels was the ninth and the last of those killed in the series of explosions.

A fourth explosion took place on Monday afternoon and a fifth explosion happened on Monday evening. It set the shaft timbers on fire as well as everything on top of the mine. No one was hurt in the final two explosions, but the toll for Cardiff was 9 dead, 13 injured, and 50 mules killed.

The mine became the tomb for three miners. Ulysis Alderson, Archie Wilson, and James Hutchinson remain buried in the Cardiff mine to this day.

Harry Parker, the mine superintendent at Cardiff, is pictured at far left just after the 1903 mine disaster. The other men are coal company officials from Chicago. Parker had equipped them with lights, jackets, and tools. They were walking toward the mine to inspect the damage when the second explosion happened. They would have been killed if they had been there a few minutes sooner. The officials gave the lights and the tools back to Parker and said, "Here, you take care of it! We're going back to Chicago!" Disheartened, Parker later quit the mining business and moved to a nearby town—Cherry, Illinois—and opened a store. He let miners buy goods on credit. If they did not have the money on payday, Parker put it on the books. Then, on November 13, 1909, a fire in the Cherry mine killed 259 men and boys. It remains the third-worst mining disaster in US history. All the men who died in the Cherry mine owed Harry Parker money. It wiped him out financially.

Hector McAllister, the state mine inspector for the first district, was born in England. He worked in British mines from the age of eight until he came to the United States in 1864. McAllister worked in coal mines in Pennsylvania before moving to Illinois in 1865. He worked in mines near Belleville and Streator until he was appointed an inspector in 1897.

Pictured above left are Richard and Elizabeth Savage and their children Mary (in back), Maggie (in front), Mary, and Tommy (on Elizabeth's lap). Richard died in the Cardiff mine in 1901. Pictured at right is the monument in Sacred Heart Cemetery in Campus for 23-year-old John McClosky, who was killed in the 1903 Cardiff mine explosion.

Ulysis Alderson (at left) was killed in the 1903 disaster. His wife, Margaret, and daughters Mildred (left) and Elizabeth (right) are pictured below in 1903. The following year, Margaret married Ralph Taylor, proprietor of the Hotel Cardiff. Margaret died in 1966 at age 84. Also killed in 1903 were James Hewitt, John McClosky, James Barra, Anton Hasal, Anton Jeokoski, Archie Wilson, James Hutchinson, and Allen Michaels. The disaster made orphans of 26 children.

Nine others lost their lives in the Cardiff mines. Matthew Brown was killed while sinking the mineshaft in 1899. Martin Cleanson was killed when he was hit on the head by a descending cage in 1900. Richard Savage was killed when he fell down a shaft in 1901. Joseph Beltram was killed in 1905 when the mine roof collapsed. Frank Passcro was killed by falling rock in 1906. Charles White died when a mule pulled a coal car over him in 1908. Joseph Ficher was crushed by coal in 1909. Adolph Monstrastello was killed by falling rock in 1909. Charles Vignery was crushed between two railroad cars in 1910.

Ulysis Alderson married Margaret "Maggie" Savage in 1899 in Clarke City. Maggie was the daughter of Richard Savage, another miner killed in the mine. When Otto Kruse and Mary Savage went to Kankakee to get married in 1904, Mary's sister Maggie and Ralph Taylor went along as witnesses. Taylor suddenly proposed, and the judge married two couples that day. Pictured is Elizabeth Alderson, the daughter of Ulysis and Maggie, in 1919 and in 1989.

Margaret (Alderson) Taylor (left) and her daughter Elizabeth (right) are pictured in 1917.

Joseph Beltram (originally Beltrami) was born in Italy in 1877. He worked in the South Wilmington mine before moving to Cardiff in 1903. He was 28 years old when he was killed in the Cardiff mine in 1905. His last words to his wife were, "Give me something so I can die." His wife gave him a shot of whiskey, and he died.

Pictured are, from left to right, the children of Joseph and Minnie Beltram, Delena, Josephine, and Peter, at their Cardiff house in 1906. The coal company allowed the family to live in a miner's shack rent free after Joseph's death.

Minnie Beltram, Joseph's 22-year-old widow, is seen here in happier times. Minnie was pregnant with Josephine when her husband was killed. The baby was born two months later. Minnie never remarried. She died in 1963. Peter Beltram (1902–1981) was a telegrapher and agent for railroads most of his life. He married Marge Guest (1911–2013) in 1930. Delena Beltram taught at the one-room Steichen School near Dwight. She married Harry Huber (1897–1994) in 1929, and they had two daughters, Donna and Gerrianne, and lived in Pontiac. Josephine Beltram became a "Harvey Girl" with the Harvey restaurant chain along the Santa Fe Railroad, primarily in New Mexico and California. She married Walter Sohan (1909–1979) in 1931. They raised three children in Joliet: Constance, Walter, and Norman. Josephine Sohan died on October 29, 2006, at the age of 100. Delena Huber died on October 24, 2008, at the age of 104.

Lorenzo Nani was born in Italy and came to America as a young man. After finding work in the Cardiff mine in 1904, he brought his fiancé, Orsolina Chelli, to America. They were married at Ellis Island. Their first son, Atillio, was born in Cardiff in 1905. Four more children were born in Cardiff.

When mining operations began closing in 1911, Lorenzo found a job in a mine in Rend City in downstate Illinois. Before he could send for his family, he was killed in a cave-in there. The family had been in Cardiff for seven years and had no where else to go. Lorenzo's last child, Lawrence, was born on November 8, 1911, in Cardiff. He is pictured on his mother's lap in 1912; on the left in front is Nando, and on the right is Oliver. In the back are Atillio and Laura.

Orsolina Nani's brother went to work in a coal mine in West Frankfort in southern Illinois. The Nani family moved there in 1917, where Orsolina ran a boardinghouse. Pictured here are Orsolina Nani and her children (from left to right) Oliver, Atillio, Lawrence, and Nando in 1918. The family moved to Joliet in 1924. By this time, she was remarried to Charles Santini, who had been a boarder at her rooming house. Santini was a musician as well as a miner and a baker. Nando and Lawrence took his last name. Orsolina died in 1955; Charles died in 1976. Lawrence Santini was 95 years old in 2007 when he came back to Cardiff for the dedication of the state historical marker. He died in Joliet on August 11, 2013, at the age of 101.

After Lorenzo Nani was killed in a downstate mine accident, his body was brought for burial in Sacred Heart Cemetery in Campus. His marker reads (in Italian, translated here), "Lorenzo Nani, died 17 July 1911, age 31. Cardiff, Ill. Left his wife with 5 children in bad circumstances."

Pictured here are Anton Hasel and Mary Vilt on their wedding day, January 6, 1896, in Coal City. Hasel died in the Cardiff mine in 1903.

Charles Vignery was the last of 18 men killed in the Cardiff mines. He died in 1910. This picture is from 1909 when he finished school in Braceville.

Charles Atherton was a mine official in Cardiff and was active in civic affairs. He is pictured here with his wife, Barbara (Dachsteiner), and four of their six children. From left to right, the children are Sadie, George, Marguerite, and Arnold. After leaving Cardiff in 1908, Atherton became a foreman at the mine in Cherry. He supervised work to repair the mine and recover bodies from the mine disaster there. Milish Manditch, a 23-year-old Austrian immigrant, was fired by Atherton on February 15, 1910. Three days later, Manditch entered the boiler room and asked for James Steele, the mine superintendent. When he could not find Steele, Manditch went to the tipple, where Atherton was pushing a car to a cage. Manditch shot Atherton several times, and he died on February 22. Barbara delivered their seventh child shortly after her husband's death. Manditch pleaded guilty to murder and was sentenced to 45 years in the state penitentiary at Joliet. Barbara died in 1934 at the age of 59.

Four

LIFE GOES ON

After the disaster, the company immediately announced it would sink a new mine shaft. Some miners left, although according to many newspaper accounts, the town still had a large and lively population. Many men stayed to dig a new mine.

The machinery for a second shaft was already in Cardiff before the explosions. The newspaper reported on April 1, 1903, "Pay day at the shaft came in regular time, and the monthly and day men were made glad."

A second mine was drilled a half mile west of the first mine. The first coal was brought up on June 7, less than three months after the explosions closed the first Cardiff mine.

Life continued as usual. Newspaper items told of couples getting married, new buildings going up, people moving into town, new sidewalks and streetlights, and other ordinary events in an ordinary town.

In January 1907, the Cardiff mine was producing so much coal that the Wabash Railroad could not haul it all. The years 1907 and 1908 were the best for the village of Cardiff and for the coal company. In 1907, a total of 216,781 tons of coal was mined, and 424 people worked in the mine and in mining operations.

Fred E. Ahern saw baseball as an alternative for the miners instead of spending time in the saloons. His F.E.A. team was considered to be among the best in the state. The team toured the state when the miners could get time off. A carload of lumber arrived in Cardiff in March 1907, and a large grandstand was built. It gave Cardiff the finest baseball park in the area.

There was such an intense rivalry between the Cardiff and Cabery baseball teams that after one game in October 1907, Cardiff mayor Frank Milem held fans at gunpoint to clear a path for an automobile of Cabery fans to leave the ballpark.

The second Cardiff mine is pictured here under construction in 1903.

This view looks north on Wabash
Avenue from Main Street.

This was Peter Juricic's Maxwell
automobile in Cardiff in 1917.

These photographs from the Tyrrell family photo album are not identified as to the events or the names of the people, but they were taken in Cardiff and were likely from a big Labor Day celebration.

The first Labor Day celebration in Cardiff was on September 3, 1900. Events included baseball games, a shooting tournament, foot races, and more. The United Mine Workers organized the day. Burch's orchestra of Fairbury provided music for evening dancing.

Minnie and Thomas Tyrrell are in the second row on the right.

LABOR DAY AT CARDIFF

Monday, September 7th Will Be Observed With Game, Sports and Speaches By Prominent Speakers.

The fourth annual Labor Day will be celebrated at Cardiff on Monday, September 7th, by the Local Union 1085. There will be games of all kinds, speaking by several prominent speakers, a grand street parade, and is the laboring man's day of rejoicing. For his success, let every one turn in and give a helping hand.

PROGRAM OF THE DAY.

Grand Parade at 10 o'clock a. m.

Sports of all kinds, games of chance, foot races, wheelbarrow, sack.

Speaking by Judge White, of Pontiac, and J. B. Wilson, of Westville.

The Cardiff Cornet Band and Cardiff Choral Society will furnish music for the day.

Dance in the evening at Choketty's Hall. Music by the Cardiff Orchestra.

100-Yard Foot Race, free-for-all; first prize, $3.00; 2d, $2.00. 5 to enter. Entrance Fee, 25c each.

Wheelbarrow Race, blind-fold; 5 to enter; first prize, $2.00; 2d, $1.00. Entrance Fee, 25c.

Potato Race, 25 potatoes; 5 to enter; first prize, $3.00; 2d, $2.00. Entrance fee, 25c.

Old Men's Race, 50 yards, over 50 years of age; first prize, $2.00; 2d, $1.00.

Boys' Race, under 12 years, 50 yards; first prize, $1.00; 2d, 50c.

Girls' Race, under 12 years, 50 yards; first prize, $1.00; 2d 50c.

Quoiting; 10 yards, 3 teams to enter; prize $7.00. Entrance, $1. per team.

Italia Boote Ball, 3 teams to enter; prize, $7.00. Entrance, $1. per team.

Run, Hop, Step and Jump, 5 to enter; first prize, $3; 2d, $2. 25c to enter.

The Cardiff Gun Club has made arrangements for a big shoot on this day, at which all the noted crack shots in this section of the state will be present. 25 bird race for a purse of $25.00. $10.00 for average shot entire program. Also other prizes for best average shots of the day.

Committee on Arrangements—F. K. Milem, Wm. Hailstone, J. J. Williams, William Hailstone, Theo. Pritchard and M. Maddin.

Committee on Sports—Ed. Murphy, John Almcrantz, Wm. Short, Geo. Goodal.

Everybody turn out and make this the biggest day of all.

Labor Day was the big holiday in Cardiff and in most coal mining towns. This poster from 1903 shows a number of activities planned for the day.

People gathered for the Labor Day festivities in Cardiff on September 5, 1910, sponsored by Farmer's Elevator.

Ben Thompson retired from farming and built this house near the blacksmith shop in 1905. A child plays on the front porch.

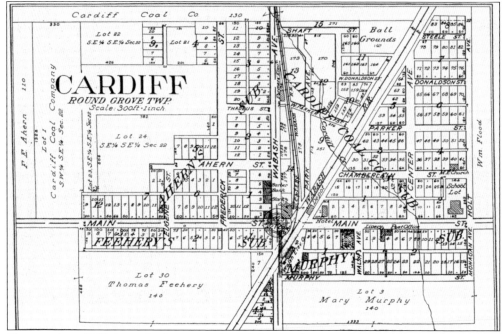

This map from 1907 shows the depot, Hotel Cardiff, grain elevators, the company store, the baseball park, church, school, and more. The subdivisions were named for the people who owned the land. The streets were named for people in the Ahern family (Thaddeus Street, Frederick Street, Eugene Street, and Ahern Street) and for mine and local officials (Parker Street, Chamberlain Street, Donaldson Street, Monaghan Avenue, Holt Avenue, Murphy Avenue, and Walsh Avenue). More streets were added later, such as Hartnett Avenue and the streets in Ahern's subdivision: Limerick Street, Shamrock Street, and Lover's Lane at Main and Frederick Streets.

This picture could be from the Labor Day holiday in 1909 or another celebration. Members of the Ciochetti family are included.

Dominic Beneitone (left) and friends enjoy a drink at a Cardiff event.

The Methodist-Episcopal Church was built on Chamberlain Street in 1902.

This house was built in Cardiff but is unidentified.

The people at this Cardiff house are unidentified.

Pictured here are the casts of two plays presented by the Cardiff Dramatic Association, *The Cheerful Liar* from March 1905 (above) and *The Gun Club* (below). Goldie Roquet (above center, in white dress) had always wanted to be on the stage, and here in Cardiff, she was.

Pictured in this image from 1902 are, from left to right, (first row) two unidentified girls; (second row) Lucy Testa and Margaret Meyers.

This was the house of Charles Wagner, a grain dealer in Cardiff. He married Martha McCleish, the daughter of John and Susan McCleish.

This was Louis Tintorri's tavern on the southwest corner of Main Street and Wabash Avenue. An advertisement for Radeke Beer, brewed in Kankakee, is on the side: "The Radeke Brew will agree with you." The building partially seen on the right was owned by Dominic Gallo. Next to that was the Rolando store.

Louis Tintorri was born in Italy in 1874, as was his wife, Jennie, in 1890. They were married in 1907. Their first four children were born in Cardiff: Minnie (1908–1952), Catherine Mackin-Webb (1909–2009), Elizabeth (1912–1995), and Louis Jr. (1916–2009). Their last five children were born in Georgetown: James (1918–2010), Dominic (1920–1920), Cecelia Reasor (1922–2016), Charles (1925–2010), and Joe (1931–2010).

Tom Z. Jones (1885–1953) was principal of Cardiff School in 1912 and 1913.

Clara Peterson (1892–1939) began teaching school in Cardiff in 1917 and later taught in Campus. Peterson was the daughter of Danish immigrants and was a sister of Mattie Ulrich of Campus.

Five

THE PEOPLE OF CARDIFF

One cannot tell the story of a town or a business or anything else without telling the story of the people who made it happen.

Cardiff had a lot of people. Many were itinerant miners who came and went. There also were several large and established families—people who built the town, who ran things, and who stayed in the area once mining ceased.

A few of the prominent names from Cardiff include Parker, Ahern, Walsh, Beneitone, Ballotti, McCleish, Ciochetti, Secondino, Scapino, Juricic, Hamill, Murphy, Bertoncello, Morgan, Humphreys, Singer, Roquet, Readdy, Regis, Lockwood, Fitzpatrick, Maguire, Crofts, Menozzi, Ronchetti, Meyers, Tyrrell, Testa, Wortman, Rolando, Vignery, Buffo, Friedberg, Cohen, Romanetto, and Biava, among many others.

This chapter tells a little bit about some of these people.

Pictured are, from left to right, Louis, Gratina, and Pete Romanetto. Louis was killed in action during World War II.

CARDIFF SCHOOL
District No. 300
Livingston County, Ill.

T. F. CLINTON, Principal

PUPILS

Nona Duke	Frances Beneitone
Blanche Carmean	Esther Carlson
Emma Hreha	Alice Treasure
Edith Coskey	Pearl Bretschneider
Marie Singer	Hazel Murphy
Hazel Kerns	Celia Baima
Carolina Wortman	Fred Jacobson
Arthur Marshall	Chas. Fox
John Secondino	Romeo Vallero
Katie Wortman	William Morgan
Rachel Hamill	Maynard James
Earl Duke	William McCully
James Higgins	Mario Vallero
Louis Secondino	Leon White
Fanny Kolling	Arthur Roquet
Frank Kolling	Patrick Devlin
Charles Secondino	

SCHOOL BOARD

John McCully	James Singer
Archie Hamill	

This is a school program from 1909, which lists many Cardiff family names.

Henry Meyers (1849–1910) operated a saloon in Cardiff for many years. The family also owned a restaurant and bakery. Henry and his wife, Theresia (1849–1914), had three daughters, Goldie, Clara, and Margaret. Clara (1883–1912) married George Falk in Cardiff in 1908. Goldie (1885–1977) married Joseph Roquet in Cardiff in 1906. Margaret Meyers (1888–1965) never married.

Henry and Theresia Meyers and two of their daughters were photographed at their home in Cardiff.

The Henry Meyers family posed in front of their house in Cardiff. Below are, from left to right, (first row) Joe Urbain, Victor Urbain, Margaret Meyers, Goldie (Meyers) Roquet, and unidentified; (on the porch) Mary Urbain, Theresia (Hasele Urbain) Meyers, Henry Meyers, and Clara (Meyers) Falk.

The Singer-Roquet family is pictured here in 1939. From left to right are (first row) Alice Singer, Marie (Singer) Roquet, Elizabeth Singer, James and Rachel Singer, and unidentified; (second row) Eloise Roquet, Arthur Roquet, Lois Roquet, Andrew Singer, Marjorie Singer, and Jean Singer. Henry Singer (1837–1904) was the first of his family to come to Cardiff. He was born in Wales, near the original Cardiff, and married Margaret Williams (1836–1912), also born in Wales, in 1859. Henry Singer worked in coal mines as a child and came to Braidwood in 1877 to work in the mines. After operating a butcher shop in Streator for 16 years, he moved to Cardiff in 1899 and opened a store. Henry and Margaret Singer had 13 children. Two of their sons, Thomas and Andrew, worked in the Cardiff mine. James Singer (1863–1941), another son, was the town constable in Cardiff for many years. He also was a butcher and hauled coal and ice. He and his wife, Rachel (1876–1949), had two children, Marie and Andrew.

The family of Emile Roquet posed for this picture in 1917. From left to right are (first row, sitting on the ground) Arthur and Harry Roquet; (second row) Bernice Roquet, two unidentified, Emile Roquet Sr. holding Gladys, Mary Theresa Roquet, Marie Roquet holding granddaughter Ferne, Melva Diehl, Georgia Roquet holding Russell, and Goldie Roquet holding Joseph; (third row) George Roquet, unidentified, Arthur Roquet, Octave Roquet holding LaVerne, and Joe Roquet holding Victor. At left is the wedding picture for Octave Roquet and Myrtle Diehl in 1910.

Emile Roquet (1854–1929) and his wife, Marie (1860–1936), were born in Belgium and came to America in 1887. Emile worked as a coal miner in Braceville before moving to Cardiff in 1900, where he opened a saloon. Emile and Marie had six children: Emile (1880–1880), Joseph (1881–1928), Emile (1883–1962), Octave (1887–1957), George (1894–1985), and Arthur (1896–1992). The first three were born in France; the last three were born near Coal City.

This was the Roquet home in Cardiff.

Joseph Roquet and Goldie Meyers had their portrait made on their wedding day, May 14, 1906, at Sacred Heart Catholic Church in Campus. The local newspaper said the wedding was the social event of the year in Cardiff.

The family of Joseph and Goldie Roquet was photographed in 1917. Arthur, who was killed at age 11 in a hunting accident, is on the left. Joseph Jr. is on his mother's lap. The girl standing in the middle is Mary. Victor and Harry are on the right. Joseph and Goldie had six children: Arthur (1907–1918), Harry (1908–1999), Mary (1912–2013), Victor (1915–1997), Joseph Jr. (1916–1970), and Margaret Ann (1919–2008). The family moved to Cedar Point in 1918 and opened a hardware store. Two of their daughters, Mary and Margaret Ann, married McCabe brothers. Mary and Louis McCabe (1906–1987) had four children: Kathleen Bollmer in 1944, Patricia Fenker in 1946, John McCabe in 1949, and Thomas McCabe in 1951. Margaret Ann and George McCabe (1917–2002) had five children: Maureen Waller in 1943, Daniel McCabe in 1947, Eileen Moore in 1949, Joseph McCabe in 1955, and Michael McCabe in 1957.

Mary Roquet is seen at left at age four in 1916 in Cardiff. She married Louis McCabe in 1943. At the healthy age of 95, Mary came back to Cardiff in August 2007 for the dedication of the state historical marker. After being diagnosed with cancer, Mary returned to Cardiff for one final visit in September 2012 with her daughters Kathy and Patti and her niece Eileen. Mary died on February 19, 2013, at the age of 100.

Marie Singer became Cardiff's postmaster in May 1915 when she was just 18. She was also a schoolteacher in Cardiff. She married Arthur Roquet in 1919. The family later lived in Streator. Marie taught school there, and Arthur worked for Metropolitan Insurance.

Marie Singer (1896–1973) is pictured above
left at age 16. Above right are Arthur and
Marie Roquet and their children, Lois
(b. 1921) and Nicole (b. 1929). At left are
George and Bernice Roquet in 1926 with
their children, Vonda, Nancy, and George.

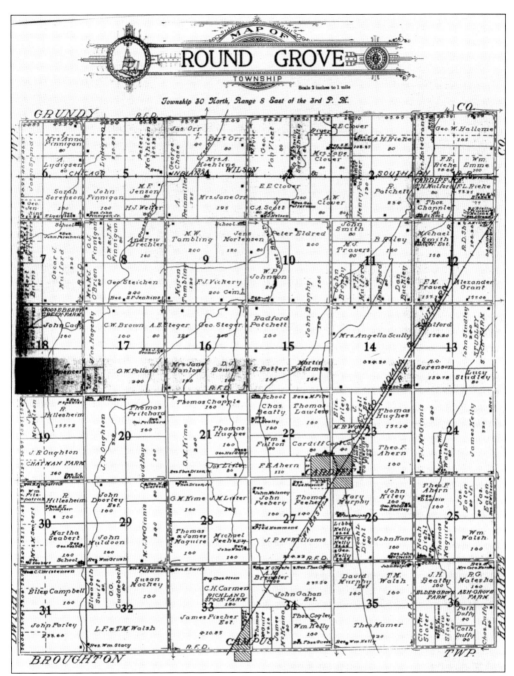

This map of Round Grove Township from the Livingston County Atlas of 1911 shows Cardiff and Campus as the only real villages in the area. Cardiff was much bigger than Campus. The map shows the Wabash Railroad line between the towns, and it shows names of property owners at the time. The now gone settlement of Wilson is also shown.

71

These Cardiff ladies are wearing the styles of the day. From left to right in the first photograph are Lucy (Testa) Monaghan, Goldie (Meyers) Roquet, and Minnie (Testa) Tyrrell and her son John in 1911. In the second photograph, from left to right, are Stella Parker, Liza (Parker) Lettsome, and Lenora (Peretti) Ciochetti in 1907.

In the first photograph, from left to right, are sisters Clara (Meyers) Falk (left) and Goldie (Meyers) Roquet. In the second photograph, from left to right, are Lucy Testa and Margaret Meyers in 1902.

Ellen Cogley married William McDonald (above left), and they farmed in Round Grove Township before moving to Iowa. In the second photograph, from left to right, are Kate, Ann, and Maggie Rolando. The Rolando family had stores in both Cardiff and Coal City.

Erminia (Ballotti) Vidano is pictured at left. In the second photograph are Polda and Steve Yattoni of Cardiff. Erminia and Polda were the daughters of John and Mary Ballotti.

From left to right in the first photograph are Mable, Esther, Bessie, and Mae Carlson of Cardiff. Above right are James H. Walsh (1872–1929) and his nephew Herbert (1897–1957) in 1900. James Walsh was mayor of Cardiff from 1909 to 1922. He married Gertrude Gifford in 1900. Walsh owned Farmers & Miners Bank in Cardiff and one of the grain elevators as well. Gertrude (1877–1937) and James had three sons: Dale (1902–1980), James (1909–1966), and Charles (1916–2007).

The first photograph shows Alf James (right) with an unidentified man. James managed the Hotel Cardiff. He went to prison in 1908 for attacking his wife with a hatchet. The second photograph shows William Diehl, who owned a livery stable in Cardiff.

Georgia Roberts (1857–1941), above left, was the wife of Thomas Roberts, the night engineer when the Cardiff mine exploded in 1903. Thomas (1848–1914) was born in Wales and worked in a coal mine in Kentucky. He and Georgia had two daughters, Ruby and Mae. Ruby (1881–1934) married John Mamer in 1904. Mae (1882–1948), above right, became a schoolteacher in Cardiff in 1903.

Delena Beltram and her mother, Minnie, are pictured in front of the second Cardiff depot building in the early 1920s.

This Milem family portrait shows, from left to right, (first row) Emma (Milem) Denhardt, Mary Ann (Kidd) Milem, John Milem, and Ida (Milem) Stohl; (second row) Frank E. Milem, John E. Milem, Mary (Milem) McCoslin, George Milem, and Caroline (Milem) Burgett. The insets are Eliza Milem and James K. Milem. Frank E. Milem was elected Cardiff's first mayor in 1900. He was elected to another term in 1907 and was president of the local miner's union at Cardiff. He was born in Cleveland, Illinois, in 1872 and came to Cardiff in 1899 when the mine opened. Milem started a saloon in Cardiff. He ran into trouble and had his license taken away in 1908. He was mayor at the time. Milem left town shortly after that. After leaving Cardiff, Frank Milem was mayor of Cleveland, as his father John had been. Frank Milem never married. He died in 1948.

Theresia Meyers, shown here, was the wife of saloonkeeper Henry Meyers.

Betty (Romanetto) Biava is pictured here.

Some of the Baima family are pictured here in 1902. From left to right are Bartholomeo Baima holding Margaret; his wife, Eugenia "Jennie;" and Cecelia with her umbrella. Bartholomeo was born in Italy in 1865 and came to America in 1888. His first job was in Coal City. The Baima home in Cardiff was a white frame, two-story house next to the railroad tracks. Bartholomeo worked in the Cardiff coal mine. Bartholomeo and Jennie had eight children: Cecelia (1897–1985), Thomas (1899–1899), Eugenia Margherita "Margaret" (1901–2000), Mary (1903–1913), Thomas (1906–1982), Anthony (1908–1977), Genevieve "Jean" (1911–1971), and Albert (1913–1943). The first four children were born in Carbon Hill; the last four were born in Cardiff. Bartholomeo died of stomach cancer in 1916 at the age of 51. Jennie died in 1929. M.Sgt. Anthony Baima was an airplane mechanic at Pearl Harbor on December 7, 1941, when the Japanese attacked. T.Sgt. Albert Baima was killed in an airplane training accident in Oklahoma in 1943 during World War II.

Battista Ciochetti was born in 1867 in Italy. He married Domenica Buffo in Italy in 1886. He had one of the biggest saloons and halls in Clarke City and in Cardiff. The name often was spelled "Chocketty" in newspaper accounts and in court records. Some family members preferred the Americanized spelling. Ciochetti died of a stroke in 1907 while on a visit to Italy. He is buried in Priacco, Italy.

Pictured here are, from left to right, (first row) John and Lucia Ciochetti; (second row) Vigga Buffo, Libra Buffo, John Buffo, unidentified, Lucia Buffo, and Domenica (Buffo) Ciochetti.

Pictured from left to right are (seated) Lucy (Ciochetti) Barbatti; (standing) James Ciochetti, Pierino Ciochetti, and Silvio Barbatti. Domenica (Buffo) Ciochetti, who married Battista Ciochetti, is pictured below. The Ciochettis arrived in America on December 16, 1886. Domenica and Battista had four children: John (1887–1938), Lucy (1894–1981), James (1896–1944), and Pierino "Peter" (1899).

John, Lucy, and James were born in Clarke City. Peter was born in Priacco, Italy, while his parents were back in the old homeland for a visit. John and Lucy were raised in America by their parents, but James and Peter were raised in Priacco, Italy, by their grandmother and their uncle. Battista Ciochetti left a life of comfort in Italy for an uncertain future in America. Battista was the son of Cavaliere Ciochetti, who was the mayor of Priacco, Italy. Cavaliere also owned a construction company that helped to build the tunnel through the mountains into Switzerland. For this work, Cavaliere was knighted by the king of Italy.

Lucy Ciochetti and Silvio Barbatti are pictured on their wedding day at Sacred Heart Catholic Church in Campus on September 29, 1908. After Cardiff's mine closed, Silvio, Lucy, and Lucy's mother, Domenica, moved to Taylor Springs. Domenica Ciochetti died of tuberculosis there in 1912.

SEEING ST. LOUIS

Lucy and Silvio opened a restaurant and bar called the Rendezvous in Taylor Springs. One of their neighbors was Liza Parker, a friend from their Cardiff days. Lucy and Silvio had one child, Marie, born in Cardiff on September 15. 1914. Lucy's brother John Ciochetti married Lenora Peretti in 1907. She died in childbirth in 1909, and later John married her cousin Nora Peretti. They had four children: John Ciochetti Jr. (1914–1918), Mary (1916–2005), Lucy (1918–2001), and Lenora (1919–1921).

Pietro Romanetto (1869–1935) left Lemi, Italy, in 1904, settling in Pawnee, near Springfield, where he worked in a coal mine. His wife, Maria (1879–1961), and their first four children followed from Italy in 1909. Pietro and Mary had nine children: Frank (1898–1970), Elizabeth "Betty" Biava (1900–1996), Gratina Allione (1902–1994), John (1904–1946), Amanda (1909–1911), James (1911–1983), Louis (1912–1944), Peter (1914–1974), and Joseph (1918–1983). James Romanetto was the first of his family to come to Cardiff, arriving in 1927 to work for the railroad. His mother moved to Cardiff in the 1930s and opened a general store and tavern on Wabash Avenue. James married Elsie Grob (1914–1970) in 1941, and they had three sons: Marvin (1942–2008), Gary (b. 1944), and Robert (1951–2010).

Betty (Romanetto) Biava, pictured here, became one of the best loved people in the history of Cardiff. She and her husband, Dominic, came to Cardiff in 1940 and opened a confectionery and grocery store. Betty operated her store for 40 years. Betty was known as a local nurse and the heart of Cardiff. From her store she not only sold candy, groceries, sandwiches and more, but she also patched skinned knees and elbows of local children who slid down the slag mountain of cinders at the old mine. The medical treatment included a free treat for the child. She started her humanitarian work as a teen during World War I, knitting sweater vests for soldiers. During World War II, she rolled bandages for soldiers and continued it for the next 50 years. She lived in the back of the store.

Dominic Biava (1898–1972), Betty's husband, was a painter. They had two children, Angela and Ronald. The old store was renovated in 1993 and became a welding shop owned by brothers Gary and Bob Romanetto, Betty's nephews.

Naureadin "Doro" Bertinetti (1879–1967) worked in the Cardiff mine. He is pictured here with his wife, Teresa, and three of their children: (from left to right) Dominic (1903–1958); John (1905–1994), who was born in Cardiff; and Annie (1901–1985). They also had Camillo (1910–2004), Christina (1912–1997), Minnie (1918–2004), and Peter (1920–1921). In 1902, while working in a mine near Suffernville, Doro would pass Teresa on his way home from the mine and would say hello. She only nodded. Finally, Doro asked her, "What's the matter? You never speak to me." Teresa did not understand what he said, but she recognized his Italian accent. They began exchanging the story of their lives. The very next day, Doro asked her to marry him. Without hesitation, she agreed. They had nine children and remained married until Teresa's death in 1966 at the age of 88. Doro died a year later at the age of 88.

Dominick Beneitone (1865–1943) and his wife, Lucy (1876–1954), were married in 1894 in Italy. Dominic came to America and brought Lucy here after settling in Coal City. They had three children: Frances (1895–1966), Mary (1898–1999), and Joseph (1901–1982). The Beneitones moved to Cardiff in 1905, where Dominic opened a general store. He also did some farming and worked in the mine for awhile. The Beneitones operated their store for 12 years. Frances was Cardiff's postmaster from 1917 to 1921, with the post office located in the general store. Frances married Benjamin Walters in 1919. They moved to Joliet, where Benjamin was a carpenter. Mary married George Lithgow (1890–1971) in 1922. He was a Dwight-area carpenter and farmer. They had three children: William (1925–1983), Harold (1933–2016), and Darlene (1935). Dominic Beneitone bought Cardiff property after the mine closed and eventually owned most of the land where the village and the mine stood. This included Fred Ahern's big house.

Dominick and Lucy Beneitone are pictured with their children: (from left to right) Frances, Mary, and Joseph. Mary lived to the age of 100.

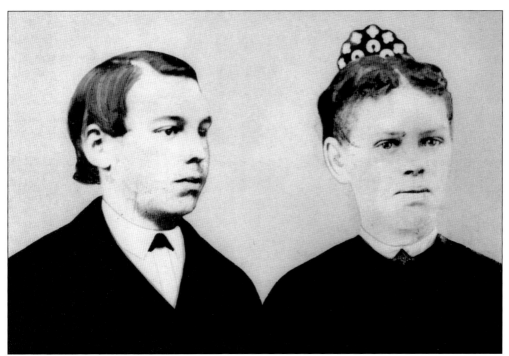

William Henry "Harry" Parker (1856–1939) and his wife, Elizabeth (1860–1941), were among Cardiff's most important people. Harry was born in England. He was the first mine superintendent at Cardiff. Harry and Elizabeth left for a few years before returning in 1915. He was named city marshal of Cardiff in 1919, and in 1922, he became the last official mayor of Cardiff. The Parkers had eight children: Ward, Robert, Eliza, Margaret, Annie, William, John, and Henry. Their house is pictured below.

William Parker, son of Harry and Elizabeth Parker, also worked in the Cardiff mine. When he was 18 years old, a pit car in the mine crushed his left foot, and he had to have some toes amputated. A carnival came to Cardiff and to Campus in 1910, and Big Bill Parker of Cardiff accepted the challenge to wrestle a bear—and he won! Below is a picture from that day, taken by Louis Ullrich.

Above are Theodore Ahern Sr. (1867–1939) and his wife, Ella (1871–1958). He was the son of Thaddeus Ahern (1812–1909), who was born in Limerick, Ireland, and was the founding member of the Ahern clan of Cardiff. Thaddeus and Bridget (1831–1890) had eight children: John, Fred, Mary, Raymond, Will, Theodore, Eugene, and Genevieve. Mary Ahern (1863–1942) married P.D. Fitzpatrick of Campus, and they had 10 children.

This was the home of Fred E. Ahern in Cardiff. The house still stands.

The Ahern house is pictured 100 years later.

Fred E. Ahern (1859–1941) was the most prominent person in Cardiff history. He constructed and owned many of the houses and business buildings in Cardiff. He founded and was president of the Bank of Cardiff, and he built and owned Farmers Elevator Co. Ahern was president of the school board and was on the village board as well. He was registered with the state as a banker and a lawyer. Ahern married Julia Doyle (who was 16 years younger and who was raised from childhood by his sister), and they had five children. His downfall began in September 1914 when he was Cardiff's postmaster and was arrested on a federal charge of embezzling $2,600. He lost his fortune when Cardiff died. Julia took the children and left him. Within a few years, Fred was sleeping in barns. During the Great Depression, Fred went to Texas with a busload of other poor people looking for work. He died in a boardinghouse in San Antonio, Texas, in 1941 and was buried in Texas. He left no kin to be notified. When Julia died in 1965, she had Fred's name carved into the tombstone in Sacred Heart Cemetery with a date of 1942. Fred E. Ahern, the most prominent man in the history of Cardiff, is not even buried in his own grave in Sacred Heart Cemetery.

Pictured at left are Harry and Jane Crofts; below are James and Lena Crofts and their children in Cardiff. Harry (1854–1913) and Jane (1848–1929) came from England in 1888, and they had four children: Robert (1877–1948), James (1879–1944), Herbert (1881–1941), and Mary Ann (b. 1882). The family settled in Central City, near Braceville, before moving to Cardiff.

James Crofts married Lena Bianco in 1905. Lena (1889–1922) was born in Braidwood to Italian immigrants Battista and Mary Bianco. The Bianco family later lived in Cardiff. The Crofts men worked in the Cardiff mine. After Cardiff's mine closed, the family moved to St. David and then to Carrier Mills. James and Lena's son Harry G. Crofts (1906–1983) was born in Cardiff. Harry married Ethel Jackson (1904–1984) in 1926, and they had two daughters, Lois, born in 1928, and Corrinne, born in 1929. Lois married Frank Trotter in 1952, and Corrinne married Jack Roen in 1949.

Harry and Jane Crofts and their grandchildren are in front of their Cardiff house in 1908. The style was typical of the modest houses in Cardiff, which were small enough to be carted away to other towns after the mine closed.

James and Lena Crofts are in front of their Cardiff house in 1908. Their son Harry G. Crofts is in the little rocking chair.

Edith Coskey is pictured at left in Cardiff in 1913 at the age of 19. Her father, Fred, was a drayman for the Cardiff Coal Co. In the second photograph, from left to right, are the McCleish brothers, Bob, George, and Bill.

This was the home of the McCleish-Vignery family in Cardiff.

Robert McCleish and Lydia Vignery were married on June 1, 1908, at Sacred Heart Catholic Church in Campus. The witnesses were Kate Flanagan and William Hamill. Robert (1889–1966) was born in Scotland; Lydia (1883–1962) was born in Braceville. She ran a millinery store in Cardiff, and Robert was a barber for several years before becoming superintendent of a mine in Harrisburg. The family moved to Pennsylvania before ending up in Brooklyn, New York. Robert was the son of John McCleish (1853–1936), who was born in Scotland and worked in the mines in Braidwood and Cardiff; he married Susan Fitzpatrick in 1877. Samuel (1878–1961), another son of John and Susan, was a barber in Cardiff; he married Cardiff schoolteacher Anna McDonald (1878–1962) in 1905. Robert and Lydia had one daughter, Ethel, born in Cardiff in 1908. Ethel married Herbert Young in 1941. She died in 2002.

The Archibald Hamill family is pictured above. From left to right are (first row) Peg, Alice, Archie Sr., Elizabeth Sr., and Katie; (second row) Elizabeth, Bill, Rose, Bob, Mary, and Archie Jr. Archie Hamill Sr. (1862–1931) was born in Scotland. He came to America and became a citizen in 1881. He worked in the coal mines at Clarke City and Braceville before coming to Cardiff in 1900. An accident in the Cardiff mine in 1904 caused most of his right foot to be amputated; however, he continued coal mining. Hamill became a school board member in Cardiff, was elected to the village board, and was head of the Local 1085 United Mine Workers union. His wife, Elizabeth (1861–1930), was also born in Scotland. They had eight children: Elizabeth, Robert, William, Mary, Archie Jr., Rachel, Alice, and Catherine, all born in Illinois between 1886 and 1902.

Pictured here are, from left to right, unidentified, Thomas J. Murphy, and Samuel McCleish.

The Thomas J. and Rose Murphy family is pictured in the 1930s. The children are, from left to right, Arch (next to his parents), Rosemary, Hamill, Allan, and Thomas W. Murphy.

Above left is Rose Hamill (1884–1973) of Cardiff at age 16. She was the oldest of the nine children of coal miner Archie Hamill. Above right is the wedding portrait of Rose and Thomas Murphy, taken on December 22, 1909, at Sacred Heart Catholic Church in Campus. Thomas and Rose Murphy had five children: Thomas W. Murphy (1910–1992), Allan Murphy (1912–2006), Rosemary Shea (1913–1995), Hamill Murphy (1917–2002), and Arch Murphy (1923–2007). Pictured below left is Laura Murphy (1916–1993), the wife of Thomas W. Murphy.

Pictured here are Margaret Lloyd and William Morgan on their wedding day on July 21, 1890 (right), and on their 50th anniversary, July 21, 1940 (below). Born in England, William Morgan (1868–1943) was a coal miner in Clarke City and in Cardiff. Margaret (1874–1948) was born in Wales.

Together, Margaret and William had 10 children: Elizabeth "Mae" (1891–1986), Frances (1893–1945), William Jr. (1896–1961), Gwendolyn (1898–1923), Rose (1900–1980), Richard (1902–1978), Arthur (1906–1993), David (1908–1985), Margaret (1910–1991), and Lloyd (1914–1914). Elizabeth and Frances were born in Gardner; William, Gwendolyn, and Rose were born in Clarke City; Richard, Arthur, and David were born in Cardiff; and Margaret was born in Chicago.

The Morgan family is at home in Cardiff in 1904. Pictured here are, from left to right (first row) Richard in the lap of Elizabeth "Mae," Frances, Gwendolyn, and William Jr.; (second row) wife Margaret, Sarah Ann Price (Margaret's sister), Rose Julia Morgan (little girl), and unidentified; (third row) William Morgan.

This was the Tyrrell farm at Cardiff. Patrick and Bridget Tyrrell left County Meath, Ireland, for America in 1869. Patrick's sister was Ann Collopy, and her farm was where Cardiff would be built. John Tyrrell (1859–1900) married Elizabeth Sinnott (1859–1927) in 1881. They had four children: Thomas Tyrrell (1883–1971), James Tyrrell, Laura Testa (1890–1967), and Mamie Tyrrell (1892–1908). Thomas married Minnie Testa (1884–1968) in 1910 at Sacred Heart Catholic Church. He became a hoisting engineer for the coal company in 1904. Thomas and Minnie had one son, John, and they adopted Anna Testa, the daughter of a relative, after her parents died.

The *Dwight Star* carried this account of the wedding of Thomas Tyrrell and Minnie Testa on January 12, 1910: "Two of the most popular young people of Cardiff, Mr. Thomas Tyrrell and Miss Minnie Testa, daughter of Mr. and Mrs. John Testa, were united in the holy bonds of matrimony at the Sacred Heart Church in Campus, Wednesday morning at 9 o'clock, Rev. M.A. Humphrey officiating. Peter Testa, brother of the bride, acted as best man, and Miss Laura Tyrrell, sister of the bridegroom, was bridesmaid. Immediately after the ceremony, the bridal party returned to the home of the bride's parents in Cardiff, where a bountiful wedding breakfast awaited them together with many relatives. The bridal couple left on the 2:30 train in the afternoon for Chicago on their wedding trip. Mr. Tyrrell is a young engineer at the coal mine and has a large circle of friends here. Miss Testa is one of Cardiff's highly esteemed young ladies. The happy young couple will reside in Cardiff."

Thomas and Minnie Tyrrell's son, John, was born on October 10, 1910 (or 10-10-10). He is pictured at right in his perambulator. John (1910–1998) married Lorraine Duay in 1961. He farmed and worked on the highway maintenance crew. He was Round Grove Township clerk for 34 years, from 1959 to 1993.

John Testa (1855–1941) was born in Torino, Italy. He married Mary Testa (1854–1939) in 1881 in Italy, and they came to America that same year and lived in Braidwood. They had seven children: Angela, Mary, Minnie, Peter, Lucy, Anton, and Philip. John worked in the mine in Carbon Hill before moving to Cardiff in 1902. He built a general store, meat market, and saloon on Main Street. After the mine closed, John and Mary remained in Cardiff for the rest of their lives. Angela (1883–1918) married William McLean in 1901. He was a blacksmith in Carbon Hill and Cardiff. Their daughter Marie married Clifford Williams, the grandson of Cardiff's mine superintendent Harry Parker. Mary Testa (1884–1959) married Caesar Antoniono. Anton Testa (1891–1963) married Geneva Kimbro (1904–1959). Minnie married Thomas Tyrrell in 1910. Peter Testa (1886–1965) married Laura Tyrrell (1890–1967) in 1911; Laura was Thomas Tyrrell's sister. Lucy Testa (1889–1981) married William Monaghan in 1908 at Sacred Heart Catholic Church. Philip Testa (1893–1975) owned a Ford dealership. He married Sylva Crum (1900–1994) in 1931.

John and Mary Testa are in front of their house in Cardiff in both of these photographs. Joining them below are, in the back, Tony Testa, Ceaser Antoniono, Merrial Antoniono, Rose Testa, Mary Testa, and Loretta (Testa) Dunbar.

Pictured above left are John and Mary Testa. Pictured above right are Elizabeth and Harry Parker and great-granddaughters Anita (left) and Angela Margaret Williams (right). The girls' grandparents were Will and Angela (Testa) McLean and Thomas and Margaret (Parker) Williams; their other great-grandparents were John and Mary Testa. Pictured below left are Will and Angela McLean in 1901. Angela was the daughter of John and Mary Testa. Angela's daughter Marie married Clifford Williams, the grandson of Harry Parker.

The Monaghan family is pictured above. From left to right are (first row) William Monaghan, William Jr., and Vyetta (Monahan) Bleser; (second row) Lucy (Testa) Monaghan and Sam Monaghan. Lucy Testa (1889–1981) married William Monaghan (1878–1950) in 1908 in Sacred Heart Catholic Church in Campus. William, who was born in Scotland, worked in the coal mines. The Monaghan house was built in 1902 on the south side of Main Street at Frederick Avenue. After the mine closed, the Monaghans moved from Cardiff to the coalfields in downstate Hillsboro in 1917. William and Lucy Monaghan had three children: Vyetta (1910–2013), Samuel (1913–2002), and William Jr. (1923–1975). Vyetta married Richard Bleser (1912–1999) in 1936, and they had three children: Richard Bleser (1938–2008), Patricia Lochner (1943–2021), and Joseph Bleser (b. 1945). When Yvetta died at the age of 102, she left two children, 14 grandchildren, 29 great-grandchildren, and one great-great-grandchild. After William died, Lucy married John Gallo (1887–1985), a childhood friend from Joliet.

Henry Ronchetti and Catherine Perona are seen at left on their wedding day, December 24, 1908. Henry and Catherine met on the ship from Italy to New York. Catherine was on her way to America to meet her fiancé. By the time the ship got to America, she and Henry were in love, and the other fellow was left disappointed. Henry (1880–1941) and Catherine (1888–1952) had four children, all born in Cardiff: Maria Hirsch (1909–2001), George Ronchetti (1911–1985), Viola Sontag (1912–2004), and Charles Ronchetti (1920–1998). Henry ran a butcher shop and grocery store in Cardiff from 1908 to 1922 and then moved to Joliet and opened a grocery store there.

From left to right, Viola, Catherine, Mary, Charles, Henry, and George Ronchetti were photographed in Cardiff in 1920.

Charles and Teresa Scapino are pictured with their children: (from left to right) Angela, John, Lena, and Josephine. Charles worked in the Cardiff coal mines and owned a bakery in Cardiff. Charles was born in Caluso, Italy, in 1876. Teresa was born there in 1878. They were married in 1899. Hard economic times led the Scapinos to seek a better life in America. Charles had an uncle who was a coal miner in Cardiff. It was common for immigrants to go where a relative already was established and where a job was waiting, so Charles came to Cardiff in December 1904. Teresa and their children followed after Charles was settled in Cardiff. When Teresa and the children got off the train at Cardiff, she did not see anyone there to meet them. She sat down and cried. A passing peddler helped her find Charles. Needless to say, whenever that peddler came to her door, Teresa always bought something from him.

The Scapino girls are pictured outside their Cardiff home in 1911. Lena holds the large doll, while Josephine (left) and Angela stand behind her. Three of the Scapino children were born in Italy, and four more were born in Cardiff. After Cardiff's mine closed, Charles Scapino went to Taylor Springs. Two more children were born there. Many miners who went to other towns to look for work did not take their families and instead waited to send for them after getting settled. Charles would not leave his family, so they all went to Taylor Springs. That is why Teresa always had boarders, men who left their families in the last town or men who had just come over from Italy. A chunk of coal in the Taylor Springs mine fell on Charles's chest, crushing him to death on March 24, 1924. The family moved to Chicago for better jobs. Teresa Scapino died on April 2, 1959, at the age of 80.

Frank and Rose Secondino, with son Peter between them and sons John (left) and Louis (right) standing in back, were photographed in 1911. Frank was born in Lauriano, Italy, in 1870. He and his brother Domenic came to America in 1892. Frank worked in a stone quarry in Joliet for a few years and then returned to Italy to marry Rose. Frank then worked as a coal miner in Suffernville, near Coal City. Two sons were born at Coal City: Louis (1896–1997) and John (1898–1993). The family moved to Cardiff in the early 1900s where Frank worked in the mine. A third son, Peter, was born in Cardiff in 1903. After the Cardiff mine closed, the Secondino family moved to Universal, Indiana. Frank had his Cardiff house moved to Universal in March 1913. Frank worked in the coal mine there, as did his son John. The Secondino Brothers grocery store opened in Universal in 1916. The store was in business for 33 years until the building burned in 1949. In the early 1940s, the family bought farmland and started farming.

The Regis family is pictured here. From left to right are (first row) Luisa, James Jr., John, and James Regis (second row) Anton, Joseph, and Domenic Regis. James was born in 1873 in Italy, where his family was servants to a duke. As servants, they did not have last names. When the family came to America, their last name was Sereno-Regis, an Italian form of "serene king," referring to their master in Italy. James married Luisa in Coal City in 1900. He was working in the Cardiff mine in 1904. There was another family in Cardiff named Sereno-Regis. One day in a Cardiff saloon, the two Sereno-Regis men flipped a coin to see who would get the name Sereno and who would get the name Regis. That is how James became a Regis. James and Luisa's first three sons were born in Cardiff. The last two sons were born in St. David, a downstate coal town where the family moved after the Cardiff mine closed. All the children had Sereno as their middle name. The family later moved to Universal, Indiana, before ending up in Joliet in the 1920s. Luisa died in Joliet in 1928; James died there in 1948.

Father Kennedy (above left) was pastor of Sacred Heart Catholic Church in Campus. Above right is Irene (Savage) Brodbeck (1901–1995) of Clarke City and Cardiff, a cousin of Richard Savage, who died in the Cardiff mine.

This is a look inside the Walsh brothers' store.

Fred E. Ahern Jr. is above left. Surprisingly, there are no known pictures of his famous father. Above right are three women from the Michael (1822–1907) and Cathryn (1827–1903) McGinnis family, Irish immigrants who farmed in the Campus, Cardiff, and Reddick area.

Michael and Cathryn McGinnis had 12 children. They are, from left to right, (first row) Lucille, Mildred, Dorothy, Catherine, and Bernice; (second row) George, Genevieve, and Rose; (third row) Thomas, Joseph, Frank, and Florence. Among the local descendants are the King, Buckley, Ruder, Dwyer, Piper, and Walsh families.

Cecelia Baima (left) and Marie Singer (right) grew up in Cardiff. Cecelia was 17 and Marie was 18 when this picture was taken in 1914 after their graduation from Cardiff's school.

The children of Thomas and Margaret Walsh are pictured here around 1900. From left to right are (first row) Clyde, Geraldine, and Herbert; (second row) Francis.

S.Sgt. Ronald Lockwood arrived in Bari, Italy, in January 1944. The citizens had been starving under Nazi rule, but after liberating the city, the Americans gave the people a chance to earn some money by making parachutes for the Allied troops. Among those looking for work was a petite 16-year-old girl named Vincenza Principi, known as Doris. As she entered the building, Doris pushed the door right into the handsome soldier, knocking off his cap. She noticed his eyes and said in Italian, "His eyes are like two pieces of sky!" He smiled and said, "Grazie." As Doris got to know the sergeant, she found out how this American with the Anglo name spoke Italian so fluently. Like her, he was raised by his grandparents. The Ballotti family in Cardiff spoke only Italian, so young Ronald grew up speaking both English and Italian. His Army job was as a translator. Ronald and Doris grew closer and were married on January 20, 1945, in Bari. They are pictured here on their wedding day.

Ronald Lockwood came home to Cardiff in September 1945. Doris had to wait until April 1946, when she and 500 other war brides (and 75 babies) sailed from Naples to New York on a special ship.

The Lockwoods moved to Joliet and lived in several houses during their 55-year marriage. Ronald retired from the Caterpillar Tractor factory in 1982. He died in 2000; Doris in 2016.

John Ballotti (1866–1944) and his wife, Mary (Tintori) Ballotti (1866–1959), are seen here on their 50th wedding anniversary at their Cardiff home. They were born in Italy and came to America in 1902. They had nine children. Their daughter Pauline (1898–1922) married George Lockwood (1883–1958) and they had two sons, Ronald and Kenneth. The Ballotti house (seen below) is one of two surviving houses from the original Cardiff.

The Ballotti house in Cardiff is pictured here in the 1940s. It stands just east of the Ahern house.

Six

CAMPUS

Campus was the "big town" where the organizers of the coal company would live while they ran the mine. Campus was also where the miners would be housed and where they would spend their money. But it did not work out that way. The miners lived where they worked. Houses and shops sprung up around the mine almost overnight, and before they knew it, the settlement was a much larger town than Campus.

The first name that was suggested for the new mining town was North Campus. It was known as North Campus for the first four months the mine was being developed, before Welshmen gave it the name Cardiff.

Campus is just a few miles down the Wabash Railroad tracks from Cardiff. Both are in Round Grove Township.

Cardiff had a Methodist-Episcopal church, but it did not have a Catholic church, so the Catholic miners and their families walked down the railroad tracks to Sacred Heart Catholic Church in Campus.

Charles William Sheldon (1839–1911) platted the village of Campus in 1880, along the Wabash Railroad line. Sheldon was born in Otego, New York. He was severely wounded in the Battle of Chickamauga in the Civil War. In 1869, he married Mary Frances Fisher. They had four children: Eliza (1870–1893), Mary Ellen (1882–1895), James (1879–1966), and Sarah (1873–1979).

Local lore has it that the town was known as Alida because Sheldon wanted it named for a daughter, but he had to change it since there already was a town by that name. However, legends often are flawed. He had a daughter Eliza, and there was no town of Alida (there was an Aledo). It was named Campus because the many trees made someone think of a college campus.

This was Elm Street in Campus in 1909, with Sacred Heart Catholic Church and rectory on the left and the convent school across the street.

This view looks down Center Street in Campus in the early 1900s.

These are two views of the J.D. Brophy department store on Center Street in Campus. The photograph below shows farm equipment being delivered in 1910.

The Brophy store is on the left, and the Walsh store is on the right.

Members of the Catholic Order of Foresters escorted Bishop Dunne from the Campus depot to Sacred Heart Catholic Church in the early 1900s for a confirmation ceremony. The grain elevator and the depot are in the background.

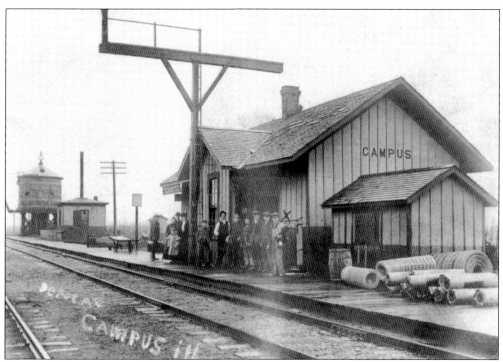

This was the Wabash depot in Campus. Section hands went on strike in April 1907, demanding a raise to $1.50 per day. They got it after a five-day strike.

This picture is identified as a Campus saloon on a Saturday night.

Bill Flood, Bill Rieck, and Julius Rieck are inside Rieck's saloon in Campus.

This novelty postcard from Campus lamented the loss of beer during Prohibition. But, of course, Prohibition did not end the consumption of alcohol in Campus or anywhere else in America. Campus had its share of the illegal manufacture and sale of liquor.

Fred McNeil was an athlete in Campus. He was also the town marshal. He is pictured here as a boxer (above left) and as a baseball player (above right) on his 21st birthday, August 13, 1903. His father, Robert McNeill, was born in Ireland. Fred married Mary Wood in 1906 at Sacred Heart Catholic Church in Campus. They had 13 children. Fred and Mary are pictured at right in their later years. Fred died in 1953, and Mary died in 1968.

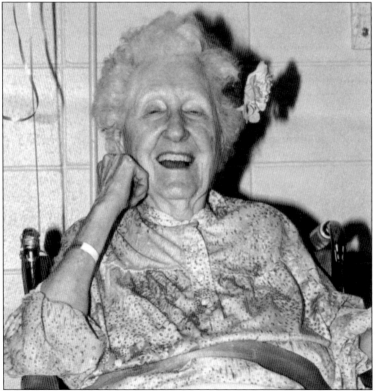

John Cody (1844-1919) was born in County Kilkenny, Ireland. He married Mary Murphy (1856-1942) in 1884, and they raised a family on their Round Grove Township farm. They are pictured above with their children, Etta, Sayde, Frank, Grover, Viola, and Nora. Etta Cody (1886-1988) was a schoolteacher in Cardiff for many years. Sayde Cody (1892-1963) married John J. Fitzpatrick of Campus. Etta is pictured at left at the age of 100.

John J. Fitzpatrick (1892–1936) was born on a farm south of Campus. He married Sayde Cody in 1924. They had six children: John J. Fitzpatrick Jr. (1925–1936), Francis Kent Fitzpatrick (1926–1936), Marietta Bennington (1927–2014), Dale Fitzpatrick (1928–1928), Bonnie Dwyer (1932–2011), and Carol Lennon (b. 1935). Fitzpatrick was mayor of Campus from 1923 to 1936. He also owned the Ford dealership in Campus with his brother Frank. There were two fatal collisions between cars and trains in Campus. On January 18, 1936, a car driven by John J. Fitzpatrick was hit by a Wabash passenger train. Fitzpatrick and his two sons, John Jr. and Francis, were killed instantly. In the second accident, seven people were killed on their way home from school on April 27, 1950, when their car was hit by a train. Killed were Mary Helen Ziehr, age 13, a seventh grader at the Campus school; Ethel McCarter, age 13, an eighth grader; Alice May McCarter, age 10, a sixth grader; Judith Johnson, age nine, a fourth grader; George Johnson, age seven, a second grader; and Barbara Seabert, age eight, a fourth grader. The car was driven by Leo Kane, who also was killed. He had driven less than a block from the school. His wife, Helen, was principal at the time. It took rescuers an hour and a half to extricate the bodies from the car. Frank Fitzpatrick was the deputy sheriff on the scene that day. It was his brother and nephews who had been killed at the same crossing 14 years earlier.

Thomas Maguire (1826–1916) came to America from Ireland in 1847 to escape the famine. He moved to Joliet in 1854 and married Mary McKenna (1833–1910) in 1861. Pictured at left, they had five children. Thomas worked on the railroad in Joliet for more than 20 years. He bought a farm in Round Grove Township. The Maguire family was the first family to register with Sacred Heart Catholic Church when it was founded in 1882. His son Thomas Patrick "T.P." Maguire (1871–1958) bought a grain elevator in the 1890s and operated it as the Maguire Brothers Grain, Coal & Lumber Company. They also operated the telephone company. T.P. Maguire was village clerk in Campus for more than 50 years.

T.P. and Lillian Maguire (1876–1955), pictured at right, had five children: Thomas (1908–1990), Kenneth (1910–1966), Dorothy (1911–2006), Eugene (1913–2001), and Ellsworth "Pat" Maguire (1917–2000). Eugene bought the Campus grocery that was started in 1891 by the Walsh brothers. The post office was in the store. Eugene and his wife, Arvilla, were postmasters for more than 30 years.

John and Ruby Mamer are pictured with their children, from left to right, Laverne, Stanton, Leland, and Ted, in 1916. Nicholas and John Mamer were two of nine children born to Theodore and Mary Mamer, immigrants from Luxembourg. Nicholas Mamer (1868–1933) married Catherine Steichen (1867–1947). John (1869–1947) married Ruby Roberts (1881–1934) in 1904. She was the daughter of Thomas Roberts, a mine engineer at Cardiff. John and Ruby had five children: Theodore (1905–1966), Laverne (1907–1981), twins Stanton (1910–1986) and Leland (1910–1979), and Helen Warnke (1919–2005). At that time, Sacred Heart Catholic Church assessed a "pew tax" in addition to regular Sunday donations. John Mamer always met his obligation for the pew tax. One Sunday, the priest mentioned John's name as one who did not pay his pew tax. This was a great embarrassment. John found the cancelled check and took it to the priest and asked him to announce the misunderstanding. The priest said he did not have to correct his mistake because it was his church. John replied that it did not have to be his church, and he left.

One of the most beautiful houses in the area is the brick house in Campus built by John Mamer in 1906 (above). It became the Walsh family house in the 1950s. Pictured at left in 1929 are John Mamer and his sons, from left to right, Stan, Ted, Laverne, and Leland. The Mamer Brothers Brick & Tile factory was one of the biggest businesses in Campus. The factory was started by Charles Sheldon, founder of the town. The business really became successful when Nicholas and John Mamer bought it in 1893.

Campus's brick and tile factory was owned by the Mamer brothers. The company's tile won a bronze medal at the St. Louis World's Fair in 1904.

The Round Grove baseball team picture in 1899 shows, from left to right, (first row) Stormy Pefferman, Bert Keeley, and Jim Thompson; (second row) Knute Mathison, James Ketcham, Mons Mathison, John Kane, and Martin Smith; (third row) ? Gibson, ? Girard, James Maguire, John Riley, and George Pefferman.

Pictured here are Francis T. Walsh (left) and his son Thomas T. Walsh (below). No other family has figured more prominently in Campus history than the Walsh family. Their importance extends from civic work to the business world. The family story started when Patrick (1821–1901) and Ann Walsh (1833–1901) came to America from Ireland in 1849, moving to a farm south of Campus in 1855. Patrick and Ann had nine children: Catherine (1862–1943), John (1859–1914), Lawrence (1861–1933), Matthew (1869–1940), James (1872–1929), George (1876–1936), Mary Mortisen, Dana Feehery (1876–1924), and Thomas M. Walsh (1866–1941).

In 1893, Thomas M. and Lawrence bought a hardware store, which eventually was expanded into a general store that included furniture, farm implements, lumber, and coal. The store housed the town's post office, and there was a dance floor on the second floor. George Walsh married Lora Gifford in 1905. They lived in Cardiff where George was a grain dealer. George was mayor of Campus from 1921 to 1923. His brother James H. Walsh had married Gertrude Gifford in 1900. Lora and Gertrude were sisters.

The Walsh's first building burned and was replaced by this brick structure across the street from the Brophy store. The street fair pictured here in 1909 was sponsored by the Modern Woodmen of America. The Campus Post Office was located in this store until it moved to its present location across the street in 1981. The Walsh Brothers Bank began in 1899. It was reorganized into a state-chartered bank in 1921 and was renamed Campus State Bank. The area with the awning to the right of the building is where the present bank was built in 1952. It is still operated by the Walsh family. Thomas M. Walsh married Margaret Sieger (1871–1959) in 1892. He was Campus postmaster from 1897 to 1914 and from 1922 to 1940, Round Grove Township supervisor for 34 years, and was chairman of the Livingston County Board. Thomas and Margaret had seven children: Philomena, Geraldine, Clyde, Francis, Herbert, Harold, and Evelyn. Francis T. Walsh (1895–1974) was president of Campus State Bank. He married Winifred Ahern (1902–2000) in 1922 at Sacred Heart Catholic Church.

The Walsh Brothers Bank of Campus is pictured in 1900. It became Campus State Bank in 1921. The Walsh family also owned Farmers & Miners Bank in Cardiff. Pictured above, from left to right, are Thomas M. Walsh, Larry Walsh, and head clerk Lowell Waybright.

Francis and Winifred Walsh and family are pictured after their wedding in 1922. At right is Winifred Walsh, the daughter of Theodore Ahern, who farmed east of Cardiff. Francis practiced law in Pontiac before moving to Campus in 1934, where he helped run the Campus State Bank. Francis and Winifred had two children: Marilyn Desens and Thomas T. Walsh. Thomas T. Walsh (1925–2009) served in the Navy in World War II. He became president of Campus State Bank. He married Joan O'Brien (1925–2002) in 1953. They had six children: Mary Margaret, Thomas M., Barbara, Cynthia, and twins John and Joan.

Marilyn Walsh (1923–2016) married Sherwin Desens (1921–2019) in 1945. Sherwin flew 90 combat missions over Europe during World War II, including leading a squadron supporting parachute and glider drops on D-Day. His P-47 fighter plane was disabled by ground fire three times, forcing him to bail out each time. The third time he was captured and spent nine months in a Nazi prison camp. Colonel Desens continued a distinguished military career before retiring in 1973. The Desens had two children, Nancy in 1946 and Paul in 1950.

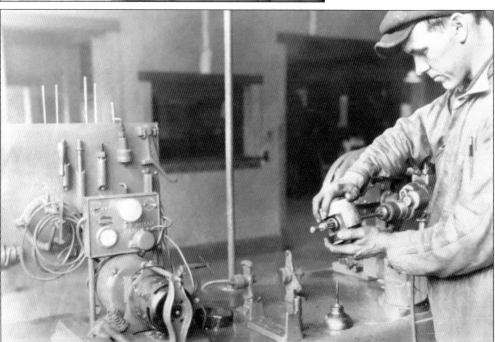

Frank Fitzpatrick works in his automobile dealership and garage in Campus in 1931.

Water fights were popular in Campus, as this one indicates in 1909.

The Ulrich family is pictured in the early 1900s. From left to right are (first row) Mary Metzske, Emma Ulrich, and Tena Smith; (second row) Henry Ulrich, Augusta Nelson, Gus Ulrich, Pauline Stacy, and Louis Ulrich. The Rieck and Ulrich families are related by marriage. Frank Reick married Amanda Ulrich, and Louise Rieck married Louis Ulrich.

The Rieck family in early 1900s features, from left to right, (seated) Julius and Fredrica Rieck; (standing) Frank, John, William, Ernest, Louise, Alfred, Julius, Edward, and Max.

The Ulrich family raised and dressed ducks for shipment to Chicago. From left to right are Ernest Rieck, Gus Ulrich, Louise Ulrich, Mattie Ulrich, Lena Ulrich, Earl Rieck, Henry Ulrich, and Ed Rieck.

Louis Ulrich, who was a very gifted amateur photographer in the early 1900s, took many pictures of his family and local people.

This picture shows Harry Goodman, an itinerant peddler and scrap salvager, on June 17, 1910, with a wagon load of rags.

Harry Goodman was photographed on May 14, 1910, taking a load of scrap iron from Campus to Kankakee.

Louis Ulrich identified this man only as "a nice old guy."

Louis (1884–1975) and Louise (Reick) Ulrich (1890–1967) were photographed on their hardscrabble farm near Campus in 1913.

From left to right, Henry Ulrich, Gus Ulrich, and Bill Metzke were photographed sawing wood with a drag saw on January 28, 1909.

The Ulrich men were photographed cutting oats on their farm.

John Ulrich is sitting at left, as Lester, Louis, Alvin, and Beatrice work on elevating corn into their barn.

Emma Ulrich and her children, Gus, Henry, Louis, and Pauline, posed for this picture in front of their Campus farmhouse.

This picture was taken on October 8, 1908, as the Ulrich men used horses to dig a ditch for a creek bed.

This is a gas-powered, six-hole corn sheller. It had been a horse-powered sheller before the Ulrich men built it into a tractor in 1936.

Henry Ulrich is shown operating the gasoline-powered engine he built in 1910 for sawing wood and shelling corn on his farm.

Louis Ulrich took this picture on August 13, 1937, when a steam engine operated by Mike Flood broke through a small bridge over a ravine southeast of Campus.

Pictured here in the early 1900s are Mike, Ed, and Mary Cuddy, and two Kennedy girls, all from the Campus area. Ed Cuddy (1887–1973) married Theresa "Tess" Farley in 1914, and they had six children: Peter Cuddy (1915–1972), Mary Tofte (1917–2001), Genevieve Derkus (1921–2013), twins Theresa Young (1925–2002) and Edward Cuddy Jr. (1925–2002), and Ann Hoffman (1933–2013).

Campus senior citizens pictured in 1938 include, from left to right, (first row) Tom Maguire, John Mamer, Dean Leffler, Tom Walsh, Mike Tyrrell, John Hamilton, and John Cassidy; (second row) Ben Hamilton, Bill Smith, Bill Breen, John Haack, Joe Tyrrell, Mike O'Keefe, and Frank Fitzpatrick.

Campus senior citizens pictured in 1938 include, from left to right, (first row) a Mrs. Cregg, Hannah Pefferman, Margaret Fitzpatrick, Mary Tyrrell, and unidentified; (second row) a Mrs. Glover, Lillian Maguire, Birdie Fenton, Margaret Walsh, Sayde Fitzpatrick, Liz Waybright, Alice Woods, Mrs. John Haack, and Mae Tyrrell.

Seven

THE END OF THE MINE AND THE END OF THE TOWN

A mine disaster of another sort hit Cardiff in 1910. The Wabash Railroad, the largest customer of Cardiff coal, announced it would stop buying Cardiff coal. The mine closed on September 21, 1912. Cardiff experienced a greater exodus in 1912 that it had after the 1903 disaster. Unlike 1903, the company did not plan to sink another mine. When the coal company left, the people left.

Newspaper columns told of families leaving town and businesses closing. Entire streets of houses owned by the coal company were moved out of town by rail.

The Cardiff Coal Company's property was sold at a public auction in 1916. The nearly 600 acres, with two coal mines, land, and buildings, brought $7,414. W.S. Burley bought 553 acres for $6,301. This included the first mine site, the baseball park, and 30 lots in town. Dominic Beneitone later became the owner of the coal mine and most of the town of Cardiff, including the fine house built by Fred Ahern.

A property on Main Street was sold by Thomas Wilkinson to James Walsh for $750 in 1910. W.H. Parker bought it in 1915 at a tax sale for $4.56. Joseph Harrison bought a property in 1933 for $150; just five months later, Harrison sold it to Dominic and Betty Biava for $1.

This sad note was in the October 27, 1923, Dwight newspaper: "Another building was moved out of Cardiff this week Tuesday. Some of the streets will be planted in corn in the spring."

The population was down to 152 in the 1920 census; the 1930 census listed just 28 people.

Cardiff's glory lasted only 13 years. But its legend as a ghost town continues—something that many people enjoy as colorful and somewhat magical.

Thank You For Stopping — Betty Biava's Store — Cardiff, III. — Phone 567-2276

This picture postcard from the 1950s shows Betty Biava's store, one of the few remaining remnants of Cardiff.

Betty Biava (left) and Katie Wortman (right) are pictured in front of Betty's store in May 1968. Katie's father, Bernard, operated a shoe and harness repair business in Cardiff. Katie lived out her days in a trailer along Wabash Avenue.

Louis Ulrich used his steam engine to move house and stores out of Cardiff in 1911 and 1912.

This was last standing miner's shack in Cardiff, photographed in 2004.

Certainly the most interesting gravestone in Round Grove Cemetery, near Cardiff and Campus, is that of Enoch Morris, who lived near Campus. He was 19 years old when he died in 1867. The stone shows the effects of time and weather and is now on the ground rather than standing. The carving at the top of the stone shows a young man leaning over, with a shotgun barrel in his mouth. The local legend is that Enoch killed himself in grief over the death of a brother who died in the Civil War in 1864. The stone reads: "Enoch / Son of James Ed & Charlotte Morris / Died Aug. 9, 1867, / Aged 19 yrs., 3 mos. / Beneath this stone the ashes lay / Of him that was my darling boy / Alas, his race is run / Caused by a double-barreled gun / Bereavements sure my heart will break / Show pity, Lord, for mercies sake / O let me to thy will resign / Those two unfortunate boys of mine." The graves of his father, James Edward Morris (1815–1890), and his grandfather Prince Morris (1795–1875) are a few feet away.

Nelson Hulse lived in Cardiff in 1906 and 1907. His family was living between Cardiff and Reddick in 1912 when a tornado on April 21 destroyed the house and killed the entire family: Nelson Hulse; his wife, Phebe; and their two daughters, nine-year-old Irene and one-year-old Bessie. A single gravestone in Round Grove Cemetery marks the burial plot for all five members of the family, including 16-month-old son Lloyd, who had died in 1906.

Another lost mining town near Cardiff was Clarke City. Quite a few men worked in the mines in both towns. This was the Clarke City school in April 1902. Among the names of students in this picture are Hutchinson, Bertoncello, Bollatto, Ballotti, and McDowell, all tied to Cardiff.

At left are Peter Menozzi (1869–1917); his wife, Giovanna (Galli) Menozzi (1876–1907); and their children: (from left to right) Emma (1904–1962), Serena (1896–1971), and Romeo (1900–1964). Peter was born in Italy and came to Clarke City in 1890. They had two more children, not pictured: Stella (1902–1982) and Clemma (1906–1997).

This is the W.H. Augustine family. Augustine was a saloonkeeper in Clarke City.

Pictured at left are John Cokley and his family. Cokley was a teacher in Clarke City and Essex and later was the Kankakee County superintendent of schools. The photograph below right is of an unidentified Clarke City family.

Pictured at left is the family of Albert Ulbrich (1882–1937). Ulbrich was a saloonkeeper in Clarke City, as was his father, August H. Ulbrich (1855–1910), a German immigrant. Albert and his wife, Frances (1892–1960), were married in 1911 and had eight children.

Pictured below left is the Clyde Dunn family of Clarke City. He was the son of William Dunn, a hoisting engineer at the Clarke City mine who later became a state representative. Below right is an unidentified Clarke City couple.

Eight

THE GHOST TOWN
LIVES IN LEGEND

Today, all that is left of Cardiff are a few remnants of sidewalks, the large mountain of waste from the second mine, and a smaller hill above the first mine. The Ahern house still stands, and there are about two dozen people in a few newer houses and trailers. Romanetto Welding is in Aunt Betty Biava's old building.

After the first book of Cardiff history was published by this author, the Illinois State Historical Society agreed to erect an official historical marker at the site. There are more than 400 historical markers across Illinois, but Cardiff is only the second one in Livingston County. The first is at Chatsworth, erected in 1954 to commemorate a train wreck in 1887 that killed 85 people.

The site includes the sign, a patio with memorial pavers, granite markers with the names of those killed in the Cardiff mines, and two benches so people traveling from a distance could sit and reflect. Cardiff was put back on the state highway map in light of the historical marker.

Sunday, August 26, 2007, was a historical day when the state historical marker was dedicated. A number of public officials and representatives from historical societies and newspapers attended. Two honored guests at the dedication were Lawrence Santini, age 95, born in Cardiff in 1911, and Mary (Roquet) McCabe, age 95, born in Cardiff in 1912.

A dedication might attract a dozen or so people. Approximately 300 people came to Cardiff's dedication. Most of the crowd stayed for hours, greeting family and friends they had not seen in years. Cardiff had not seen anything like this day since the mine closed.

On February 3, 1924, Christina White of Kankakee visited Cardiff with daughter Lara, son James, and his wife, Dorothea. Christina White was the sister of Ulysis Alderson, one of the miners killed in 1903. The Whites came to see the monument that was to have been erected where Alderson and two other miners remain entombed. They were disappointed that there was no monument. Finally, 83 years later, there is a monument.

This picture of the slag pile, or mine dump, at Cardiff was taken in the 1950s. The state seeded it with scrub brush in 1983. This large mountain on the flat prairie has been a favorite spot for people to climb.

This Cardiff sidewalk remnant was photographed in 1982.

Doris Lockwood (left) and her daughter Paula (right) attended the dedication of the state historical marker in 2007.

Mary (Roquet) McCabe (left) and Lawrence Santini (right), who were born in Cardiff 95 years earlier when it was a village, were honored guests at the dedication of the marker in 2007.

Signs were placed in 2007 to direct visitors to the memorial. The Cardiff historical memorial is approximately where Cohen's store was located.

Pictured at the dedication are, from left to right, Jim Ridings of the Herscher Area Historical Society; John Weck, president of the Illinois State Historical Society; state representative Careen Gordon; Mary McCabe; Lawrence Santini; and Patricia Wagner of the Herscher Area Historical Society.

This is the Illinois state historical marker and memorial patio at Cardiff.

DISCOVER THOUSANDS OF LOCAL HISTORY BOOKS
FEATURING MILLIONS OF VINTAGE IMAGES

Arcadia Publishing, the leading local history publisher in the United States, is committed to making history accessible and meaningful through publishing books that celebrate and preserve the heritage of America's people and places.

Find more books like this at
www.arcadiapublishing.com

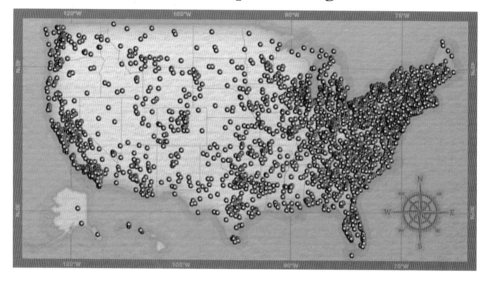

Search for your hometown history, your old stomping grounds, and even your favorite sports team.

Consistent with our mission to preserve history on a local level, this book was printed in South Carolina on American-made paper and manufactured entirely in the United States. Products carrying the accredited Forest Stewardship Council (FSC) label are printed on 100 percent FSC-certified paper.

MADE IN THE